To Cheryl
with love
from K. Dick &
God Bless!

Cry a Little, Laugh a Lot

Cry a Little, Laugh a Lot

Mary Jo Tanksley Frazer

Zondervan Publishing House
Grand Rapids, Michigan

All poems are written by the author's brother
Perry Tanksley,
who has authored twenty-five inspirational books.

Daybreak Books are published by
Zondervan Publishing House
1415 Lake Drive, S.E.
Grand Rapids, Michigan 49506

CRY A LITTLE. LAUGH A LOT

Frazer, Mary Jo Tanksley.
    Cry a little, laugh a lot.

    1. Christian life — 1930—   . I. Title.
BV4501.2.F756   1985   242   85-1578
ISBN 0-310-45510-3

85 86 87 88 89 90 / 10 9 8 7 6 5 4 3 2

The burdens that bear down on your soul
are sometimes the magic of God.

Contents

Foreword

Two things, belly laughter and tears, are essential to my sense of well-being. Whatever precipitates these emotions comes in different ways and different amounts to all of us. And each of us responds differently, according to our understanding of ourselves and the situations. Most of us, including myself, however, prefer a few tears and a lot of laughter.

The letters to my deceased parents came as the result of my seeking help while suffering unrelenting grief after their untimely deaths. When I sat down to write to my brothers and sisters to seek comfort, I was overcome with a supernatural urge to write to Mama and Daddy.

Thinking I may have grieved myself into a state of mental disrepair, I wept uncontrollably.

After the tear bath, I proceeded to do what I knew I had to do. In one sitting my soul was purged as I rapidly wrote from the well-spring of my soul.

Letter-writing and story-telling are catharses for the emotional flares of many people, among whom I am at the top of the list.

If you are comforted, made to laugh, or feel the need to purge your own soul, I am gratified.

God Bless Our Home

You can purchase a house.
A home you cannot buy,
And the reason is obvious
If a person asks why.
A house is built of wood.
A home is built of love.
A house from earth arises.
A home comes from above.
People draw plans for houses.
A home is planned by Christ.
A house is very costly.
A home cannot be priced.
Where love and kindness dwell
A house of wood and stone
Is transformed, miracle-like,
By Christ into a home.

Houses and Homes

When Edgar A. Guest said "It takes a heap o' livin' in a house t' make it home" I believe he was speaking from experience rather than observation.

After being away from our house for several days, my husband drove in the driveway with a joyous shout: "We're home." One of our children, who was less than six at the time, shook his head negatively and commented, "We're not home. This is our house. Our home is inside." We responded with glowing faces and swelling pride that only other parents can understand.

Inside, we celebrated the realization that our home is where we share our love and live together in a meaningful way. It is a place of peacemaking where God is always present. He graces our meals, heals our hurts, comforts us in our loneliness, guides our thoughts, and helps us to help others. We felt surrounded by the cozy warmth of something so invisible yet so real. Because in this same place we cry, argue, fight, forgive, play, laugh, yell, work, sleep, and often entertain friends and relatives.

"A heap o' livin'" was going on in the house we occupied, and because of what our small child said, we were awakened to an even better quality of living. We had helped a child distinguish between a house and a home, so we worked even harder at having a comfortable, clean, and inviting house and a cozy, warm, Christ-centered, happy, forgiving, and fun-filled home.

Our home is sacred and a dwelling place for God.

My Mother's Faith

Your faith in me, Mother,
Has inspired me to be
Much more than I had planned
Had you not trusted me.
Just knowing you expected
Courage from me in life
Has helped me stand my ground
When cowards fled from strife.
Your prayers for my success,
And faith I would arrive,
Put me deep in your debt
As long as I'm alive.
Mother, I often say
Whether I lose or win,
Your faith pulled up my average
From what I might have been.

Dear Mama

Dear Mama,

It seems strange that I am writing you now, but there are so many things I must tell you. Through the years, I always liked to write letters, and surely you thought at times I had very little to say. On the other hand, I caused you much worry as I told you my troubles. All the while I thought you would never die, and I was waiting for the right moment to tell you how much you really meant to me. Evidently, I didn't take advantage of my opportunities and now that you are gone, I'm left with memories and a great desire to talk with you. Even though I'm late, I will purge my soul by writing you one more time.

I suppose I should thank Daddy that I was born female, since geneticists tell us it is the male member of the human mating team who determines the sex of the child, but I want to thank you for making me feel *proud* of being a female.

Having a girl baby after three boys was very exciting to you and Daddy and your friends and relatives, but shocking to the boys.

Somehow, I seem to remember all the attention I received, and everything was pink. Do I remember that, or do I remember being told about it?

There are so many things I remember from my early years, and *nearly* all of them are pleasurable. Let me put it this way: Things that hurt weren't pleasurable, but my overall memory is of happy days growing up. There were injuries and punishments that didn't feel so great at the moment, but now when we six brothers and sisters get together, we laugh about most of them. In fact, I have very happy memories because no one told me I wasn't supposed to be happy. No one told me we were deprived or that we were living below average standards of those days. Maybe I remember the happiness better than the sadness, or perhaps I learned early that something good comes from bad situations. You taught that to me.

I recall the death of my baby brother who died of pneumonia at the age of six months. I was only three years old, and I didn't understand how broken-hearted you and Daddy were. I do remember the tears and the surrounding love to all of us by friends and relatives. That was my first lesson in sorrow and loss, as well as in the healing power of love.

We lived a good distance from Fayette, but our home on a gravel road between Blue Hill and Red Lick was the crossroads of the world to us children. I'm sure it was the boonies to you, though. You were forever listening for the motor of a car and you flagged down whoever was behind the wheel to ask him or her to take a message to someone, to deliver something, or even to give you a ride to town to get necessities. It was an inconvenience for you, but we looked forward to seeing whoever would stop next.

Many times the sound of a motor meant company. We always hoped it was a rich relative bringing gifts and good things to eat or someone with a car or truck loaded with children to play with us. We had good times playing our own kinds of games: pasture baseball, hide and seek, and others too numerous, and perhaps too dangerous, to mention. I'm sure you loved those times when we were out of hearing and sight. Most of the time you made us stay close to the house because you were unsure of our safety in the woods. Ironically, we were very close to the house and very quiet when my brothers decided to play funeral. They meticulously dug a grave without your knowledge and made it to the exact measurement of their only sister. I remember how they coaxed me to lie down in my grave and how heroic they made me feel even though I wasn't promised a reward, not even life after death!

Nothing short of "mother's intuition" brought you to the scene of the burial just as they were placing the wild flowers on the heap of dirt.

After you rescued me, I did feel heroic because the boys were switched with nobby peach tree branches, and I was simply glad to be alive. I'm sure they will never tell why they did that, but I have my ideas.

You did a good job of giving us an O.K. feeling about ourselves. But the time you and I and "Papa" were in a near fatal auto accident I certainly didn't feel very "O.K." I remember those days in the hospital in Natchez when I was given so much attention as an injured child. I was still unaware, though, that you and "Papa" were critically injured and scarred for life.

You hardly had time to recuperate. With four children, each a year apart, you couldn't stop being a mother. When we came home from the hospital you made me feel so good by teaching me, a five-year-old, how to do the housework. I have fond memories of standing on a chair by the old wood-burning range stirring whatever needed to be stirred. At your direction I put a pinch of this or a dash of that into whatever I was stirring. I still cook that way. Those who knew said it was awfully dangerous to allow a five-year-old to stand on a wooden chair by a hot iron stove. You even allowed me to start the fire in the stove after I gathered the kindling left after Daddy and the boys cut wood. Sometimes I picked up the doubleblade ax and chopped wood for myself, even though I was afraid I would cut off a foot or swing the ax back too far and bury the blade in my head.

You taught me to sew, and I made my first dress when I was seven. All the while you remade other people's clothes for me, and I felt quite proud of what we did.

When we planted a garden (which seemed to have rows 100 miles long), I usually ate more peanuts than I planted. I hated setting out tomato plants because you could always find the ones I had broken and had tried to stake up with a heap of dirt. Daddy and the boys planted cotton fields and cultivated the crops and, before the cotton had to be picked, you and I and whoever else would lend a hand canned hundreds of jars of produce from the garden. We all took turns milking Sultana, the cow, even though we really didn't like that job. Often, we faked weak hand muscles, believing you would rather milk the cow than listen to the complaints. Nothing short of famine, however, stopped my egg-gathering job. I remember the day we were forced to kill our only hen for dinner. The times that followed were very hard.

My neck and back still hurt when I think of picking row after row of cotton and of trying to keep up with you. You never seemed to tire. My sack would fill ever-so-slowly, but I was elated, even though dragging it along strapped over my shoulder got to be a chore as it filled to about 50 lbs. I tried hard to be a good "cotton picker," but you had me beat by far.

It's fun to recall those hot summer days in Mississippi and how we looked forward to the ice truck making its route through the countryside two days a week. We would race out to the truck and climb in the back where hundreds of pounds of ice blocks were covered with a tarpaulin. Lee, the ice man, sawed the fifty-pound block of ice that fit in our icebox, speared it with his tongs, and delivered it to the house. You let us play in the truck in what we called "snow" until he returned. Then Lee let the four of us sit on the tarp-covered blocks of ice and ride two miles to the home of our favorite aunt, Aunt Mary. I loved her large house with its wrap-around porch and the swing with chains that seemed to reach to the stars. We had two hours before Lee came by on his return trip, so we would swing until our feet touched the ceiling. What exhilaration. I thought it must be like flying in an airplane.

You knew Aunt Mary would serve us something good that she had baked, and she always sent something home with us as well. Many times she trusted us with eggs, buttermilk, homemade butter, cake, and pie. She often took our measurements, and when we returned she fitted a garment on us. Sometime later we took home a new outfit. She loved us country urchins, and showed it! We always had a wonderful time at her house.

All too soon for us, but probably not for you, Lee would blow the horn for us to return home. You never knew how near to danger we always were and how often we fought in the back of that open truck. And, oh, I forgot to tell you about getting our tongues stuck on the ice. That hurt! The guardian angels must have saved us for this day.

I haven't forgotten the times we were sick with malaria and other maladies. You doctored us back to good health by every method you knew. I soon learned that quinine, turpentine, kerosene, castor oil, and Vick's salve, along with a spoonful of sugar and a few other things, healed cuts, bruises, stomach aches, coughs, colds, and maybe even laziness. To this day, I can't drink orange juice without declaring that I smell and taste castor oil. I thought orange juice naturally followed the foul stuff. Yuk!

Castor oil reminds me of our outdoor "plumbing." I still wish you had persuaded Daddy to build a four-holer as our family grew! I remember some anxious moments when the two-holer was occupied and when we were down to the last few pages of the Sears Roebuck Catalog. Dad always said, "Use it all but the saddle page section. Those pages are too slick." He was right!

The best time of your life, it seems, was every year between September and May when the school bus picked us up each morning and didn't bring us back until afternoon. Perhaps our absence gave you a little time to think. But you never forgot to make us something special so we would look forward to coming home. The smell of tea cakes baking always welcomed us when we returned. How I loved to dunk them in a glass of milk. I remember how we always lingered longer than necessary at this pleasure, hoping to postpone or avoid the inevitable evening chores.

When I was six years old you had a baby girl and another when I was eight. To me they were like two real live dolls. You had too much to do, so you taught me how to care for the "babies," and I was very proud of myself. Looking back, I suspect you were glad to have me as a babysitter, even though that word wasn't in use then. Sometimes I got very tired, but I always knew you were even more tired.

I'm sure you knew of our love for you, especially the one Mother's Day when we bought you a big sack of licorice candy because we loved it so — you hated it.

You allowed me to miss school sometimes on Monday to help with the wash. There were three zinc tubs, two rub boards, and a black pot of boiling lye water in the backyard. After taking the clothes through the washing, boiling, and rinsing cycles, we starched almost everything, then hung it all up to dry. The wind would blow the sheets and cause a popping sound while everything else was stiffening. I loved the fresh clean smell, but I didn't love the ironing that lasted 'til the next wash day.

Our cistern, I recall, wasn't quite adequate except during the fall and spring rains. I remember all the times we had to haul water in drums on a truck from a relative's well or from the creek to do the wash. And I remember how we saved the water for baths! Everyone preferred the rinse water because it was cleaner, but if we argued too long and loud, you or Daddy would threaten to put us in the wash pot where the white clothes had been boiled in lye water. That was the same as saying, "I'll peel your hide." Fortunately, no one was bathed in the wash pot.

There's one thing about the cistern you never found out about, though. When the cistern was full after the rains and you requested that we get water for you, we four would take off the wooden top, draw the water, and then stand around our reflections and spit at our images to see whose shot made the largest circle. I'll bet you're glad you never knew that.

It hardly seems possible, but from the time I was born until I was twelve, our country went from the Great Depression to the Second World War. Daddy wasn't making a living for his growing family on his W. P. A. job, and our farming and gardening were hardly sustaining. You didn't have to tell us; we knew things weren't right. I'll never forget how suddenly you decided to take our meager belongings and load them into someone's small, gated truck. You even put the cow in the truck along with the boys. The rest of us rode in the cab, and off to the capitol city we went.

We stopped on Capitol Street to get a newspaper to read the classified ads and, while we were stopped, the cow escaped. Jackson was no small town, so we created quite a scene chasing a jersey cow named Sultana down the main street. It was a less than ideal way to make our debut. We finally got both the cow and the paper, along with many laughs and stares, and away we drove to a quiet spot to read the ads.

We rented a place before dark, which was a miracle because not too many people wanted a cow in their yard. One of the boys discovered an outside water faucet — the first he had ever seen — and after turning it on screamed to all of us, "We have electric water." We didn't know what electric was yet.

Nostalgia overcomes me as I think of that great move. But none of us knew how traumatic it was until many years later when we studied sociology and psychology in college.

It's fun to go back over some things, and there is much more to tell, but that's not why I'm writing. Right now I'm feeling terrible that I never really told you how much you meant to me. I never really said, "Mama, I love you." Oh, I showed it, and you knew it; but why didn't I just spend hours telling you how much I appreciated all you did?

Forgive me for the times I stuck out my tongue and made faces to your back. Sometimes I thought you were very unfair and mean. You were too strict; and, of course, I was sure you did not understand me.

After I established a home of my own and became a mother, I had new and different feelings about you, Mama, but I still had not learned to cuddle up to you and say thank you for all the sacrifices you made for your children. Your life was hard.

I never gave you credit for channeling me in the right direction, which eventually led me to commit my life to Christ. Since I was fourteen years old, I have tried to follow God's will for my life, and you deserve the praise for that.

You saw to it that we were in Sunday school and church at every opportunity. We all remember the family prayer times in the evenings. Our "funny brother" loved to select the Scripture with all the begats in it when it was his turn to read because he wanted to make us laugh. You managed to keep Daddy and all of us together until one by one the men went to serve our country. We all worked, and you told us to keep pressing forward. I don't know how you stood the pressure.

You lived to see all your children become Christians and establish Christian homes, and how excited you were when Daddy too decided to follow Christ. What a changed man! Then you both witnessed the many degrees and honors bestowed on your children. You were poor in worldly goods, but, oh, so rich — incalculably rich — with things money can't buy. And think what you left the world.

More than anything else, I wish I had said to you on every visit, in every letter, with every phone call, "Mama, I love you very much." I still have your old phone number in my book, and I know it by memory. Many times I'm tempted to call you and chat; but, of course, I know you aren't there. I'm sure you knew I cared and appreciated and loved you; but it was dumb not to say it and say it often.

Heaven and earth are full of glory because of your life, Mama.

Since I know you are resting in peace, I will forget about the unspoken words of yesterday and I too will rest in peace, believing that you now know,

"Mama, I love you."

My Daddy

Conveying love in words
Of metaphor and symbol
Is as impossible as holding
The ocean in a thimble.
Yet attempting to express
The love of a lifetime,
I attempt the impossible
In metaphor and rhyme.
Since years diminish not
The love of a child for a man,
Even now on my shoulders
I sense your guiding hand.
When distressed by uphill paths
And when my steps aren't steady,
I find strength in our friendship,
That's why I love you, Daddy.

Dear Daddy

Dear Daddy,

I think of you very often, and I only wish we could visit just one more time. The last photograph taken of you and Mama only a short time before your death sits in a frame on my dresser. I look at it often and think of you each time. My first thoughts are of your illness in those last days, but my mind loves to journey as far back as I can remember you.

You were twenty-seven years old when I, your fourth child, was born, so I don't have any recollection of you before you were thirty years old. Since we lived only a short walk from your parents, I was able to ask enough questions to get acquainted with who you were before I knew you.

I'm sure you remember when your first-born gave the names "Mamee," and "Papa," to your Mama and Papa. All the grandchildren who followed called them by those names.

We could see their large house on the hill just a

"stone's throw" from ours, and our constant plea was "May we go up yonder?" We affectionately called our grandparents' home "up yonder" until we moved away, and then we called it "down home." I still love to go "down home." Even though things aren't exactly as I remember them, it's fun to visit relatives who still live there.

I remember when we used to walk barefoot up the road to Mamee's and Papa's. We usually went around noontime because we knew that was about the time the rural mail carrier, Mr. Dent, would stop and leave the Jackson Daily Newspaper and occasionally the local weekly, along with mail order catalogs, samples of cosmetics, sticks of Wrigley's chewing gum, and other "goodies." I remember how we stretched out on the floor of the front porch and shared the funnies and other things, but we dared not touch Papa's part of the paper — the crossword puzzle. I learned then that he was a brilliant, stately Englishman and an elected public official. I looked up to him. During those summer mail calls I also learned that he grew a wee bit impatient with our questions and bickerings. We could make him happy, though, if we challenged him to a game of anagrams. He was hard to beat on the word games.

On many occasions Mamee would give us an old picture album to enjoy. How we laughed! Yep! You were pictured there as a baby in a long white dress and as a little boy with your black playmate, Jabo, who you always said was your best friend. By way of pictures, we watched you change, and we laughed each time we turned a page of the album. You looked so dapper standing by your first car. I could sense your piety even in the pictures. You were seldom pictured alone. The young beautiful girls seemed to gravitate to the tall, handsome young man with a car. Then we found you in the picture book with the most beautiful girl in the world, who later became Mama to us.

When we were young it was difficult for us to realize you could ever have been anything but a grown man. Through our inquisitiveness, however, we eventually learned about you as a boy. Mamee and Papa answered most of the questions we asked, although sometimes their answer would be "Don't you think it's about time you go back to your house?" I would usually ask if I could hold the glass Dazey churn on my lap and turn the handle 'til the butter was made. Then I'd run along home.

On one occasion, Papa told us you were a restless child with an inventive mind. He said you were a "jack of all trades" and what you didn't have you would invent or create. With more than a little disgust, he told of the gorgeous four-poster spool bed that you and Jabo sawed down to the "nubbins." Apparently you saw more value in wagon wheels than in a beautiful piece of furniture. He said the two of you sawed off every spindle and made little toy wagons for everyone on the plantation.

It frightens me even now when I think of the stories I heard about you riding through the countryside at top speed in your Ford Roadster. They say you went around the curves on two wheels.

I could recall many more stories of your life as they were told to me by various persons, but I want you to know I am more impressed by the valedictory speech you gave upon graduation from the academy than by anything else I know about you. You never knew all your children would one day have a copy. I wish I had told you what a masterpiece you delivered.

You probably never re-read or even thought about that speech after you delivered it, but it could have been spoken today because it is still so valid and important. I like to recall excerpts from that great speech:

IDEALS

(Adapted from a speech given in the spring of 1921 by Lawrence W. Tanksley.)

There are few factors more vital in a person's plan of life than his ideals. It is indeed practically impossible for a person to reach young adulthood without absorbing certain ideals of life and conduct. Every man is two men: the man he is and the man he may be. On the one hand, he is the sum total of his thought and actions in the past; and, on the other hand, a bundle of possibilities.

Dr. Katherine Blackford in a questionnaire asks the applicant, "If you could have any position you wished for, what would it be?" She says that a man's ideals are the most important thing about him; that they do more to determine his success or failure than anything else in his character.

Have you ever thought, the world's dreamers have been the world's doers? Without a clear-cut mental picture of the thing to be achieved, no man will hold on in the face of scorn and ridicule.

When young Disraeli arose in the British Parliament to make his first speech, he felt keenly the atmosphere of laughter and scorn, but he was undaunted. At the height of their ridicule he cried out, "The time will come when you will hear me!" The English Parliament was unprepared for this remark. But Disraeli held on to his dream until, as Prime Minister of England, he became one of the most highly respected statesmen and orators in the Empire.

Thomas Carlyle thought in terms of the books he expected to write and lived to reap a literary harvest. His friends ridiculed his dreams of authorship. They could not understand the aspirations of a young man who was very poor, but Carlyle assured them that he had better books in him than had ever been written.

It is important to distinguish clearly between wishing for success and having a definite, clear-cut picture of the object to be achieved. Success never comes anywhere of its own accord. Our capacity of achievement is exactly measured by our ability to imagine. One writer has said, "If your rain barrel is constructed to hold forty gallons of water, the rain clouds may send one hundred gallons into it, but it will spill out every drop beyond its capacity."

The greater men have learned to expect in larger units. Some men may be said to be almost without ideals. They possess the knack for sitting back in the last row and watching others pass by; they can see the romantic, the possibilities in other people's lives, but cannot see themselves.

Daddy, I cry when I read your words that say every man is two men. That's so true, and I see you there: the man you were and the man you could have been. You see, I have the advantage of seeing your life from beginning, as it was told to me in stories and in pictures, to end, as I saw and remembered you to your death. You were brilliant, daring, inventive, handsome,

33

generous, and extremely witty. You kept us laughing. Whenever people were in your presence, they seemed to linger for the medicinal value of the laughter that always followed your antics. Family gatherings were blah if you weren't there. Now that you are gone, many have told me how much they miss the laughter that only you could create. I miss it too, Daddy.

You taught me to drive a car. The way you taught me doesn't at all resemble the way my children were taught in driver's education. When you acquired a 1930 Dodge, I recognized that it was in excellent condition, but I was slightly embarrassed to drive a fifteen-year-old car. Yet I was willing to do almost anything to learn to drive. One easy lesson did it. I got behind the wheel, and you told me to start the car and get going. I did each thing as you instructed, and after a few miles of jerks and bumps and very abrupt stops, and maybe a few bad words, we returned home safely. You told me to drive any time I wanted, but you never mentioned a license. Someone told me I should get a license as soon as I was fifteen. You knew that was the Mississippi law, but you must have forgotten to tell me. Even though I drove a year without a license, I went to the office of the Highway Patrol and applied.

I was ecstatic when I received that very special piece of paper acknowledging me as a legitimate driver. I ran to my car, which was parked very close to where I had entered the building, because I wanted to rush home to tell you I had passed the test. In my haste and excitement, I backed into a patrolman's car and tore off the bumper. Of course, the crash brought what appeared to be an army of patrolmen running to the scene. Among them was my examiner. I was frozen with fear, but I appeared to be thawing because I covered the place with tears. The examiner recognized me and inquired about how I had arrived to get my license. I told the truth, and I believe he was so taken by my briny confession that he let me go home, but only after a lecture.

Daddy, you weren't upset when I told you about my entanglement. You said I was a good driver. Those words of assurance and my license were all that mattered at the moment.

Many of my memories of you have to do with motor vehicles. When you were discharged from the Seabees in the mid-1940s after peace was declared, you had veteran's rights to buy surplus army vehicles. I remember the jeep, the reconnaissance car, and the two-and-one-half-ton weapons carrier you bought. You gave me one lesson for all three and said that was all I needed. Since the older boys were gone from home and we lived a distance from the city bus line, I was forever needing a ride to something. I felt important and special driving the jeep and reconnaissance car to school, and my friends loved to ride with me.

On one occasion you were away from home, and I needed a ride to the Sunday night youth meeting at our church. Since I was president of the group, I decided I must go even though the only vehicle that would run was the weapons carrier. It was more like a train than a truck, but the machine-gun nest on top gave its true identity. It appeared to be as long as the lane from our house to the highway. You had told me how to get it out of the driveway so the rear end would follow the cab and not go off the narrow culvert as I crossed the highway. With both lanes clear, I drove out onto the highway with ease and then began to shift gears. I don't think I finished shifting by the time I had driven the ten miles to church. And it took almost a country mile to park the thing.

I was exhausted, but I felt heroic driving a weapons carrier with "umpteen" gears. After our meeting, the group came out to see the monster truck and to watch as I headed home. Among the onlookers was a young man I liked, and I hoped he liked me. As I started my shifting routine, the loud sound of the motor drowned out the cheers of my friends. I looked in the rear-view mirror and decided then, with a very un-okay feeling, that guys don't like girls who drive weapons carrier trucks with machine-gun nests on top. But I comforted myself as I drove out of sight by telling myself I didn't like guys who didn't like girls who came to a church meeting by the only available means, even if it was a two-and-one-half-ton truck. For a short time, I felt very okay.

I arrived at my lane, but it was not as easy to make the sharp turn *into* the narrow drive as it was to turn *out* of it. Whatever went wrong caused me to hit a utility pole. The pole snapped and wires fell across my machine-gun nest. It looked like full-fledged war as the sparks began to fly, causing a fire which spread through a huge field of broom straw. Fortunately, a passerby warned me to stay in the cab of the truck. He summoned the fire department and others, and in a short time, which seemed like years, I was rescued.

Daddy, you weren't there when that happened, but you surely heard about it later. Once again, you thought I could handle anything. You really put too much trust in me, or were you too busy with what you were doing?

You were some kind of man. I believed you qualified for nearly every profession, and that you could do anything you set your mind to do.

Right now, though, I want to forget about the man you were and think about the man you finally became.

As you said in your valedictory address, you were a man with a bundle of possibilities. As I look back, I can see that you started life with ideals to match those possibilities. But early in the journey you set out upon life's sea without a sail. You didn't have a master plan for your life, and you later confessed you certainly didn't have The Master.

We knew you cared about your family. You expressed a great amount of pride in the accomplishments of your children. We knew you loved us, and you had hope for our future; but you were obviously bogged down in life. In fact, you couldn't cope with it normally. With all your possibilities and creative genius and restlessness, you chased after shadows that left you groping in darkness.

I'm sure you remember when I witnessed to you of my personal relationship with Christ. You seemed to think that was "right nice" for women and children but not for you. You said, "Somebody'll have to prove to me that there's a God and Christ."

Daddy, I prayed for you nearly every day. Sometimes I was impatient with God because I wanted a Christian daddy immediately, one who was living up to his high ideals and possibilities. Being a daddy is difficult, and I wasn't always aware of the frustrations you must have felt trying to support all eight of us. But I was aware that you were trying to run your life all by yourself.

37

I'm sorry I didn't tell you how great you were. And I'm sorry I didn't overlook your faults and give you an emotional lift when you were down. That seems to be the irony of life. I can see it that way only now. You needed love, understanding, and the warm touch of your children's arms around you as you struggled without a savior. If I'm feeling guilty now, how guilty you must have felt then.

Cheer up! I'm saying that to myself and to you because, in the jargon of your grandchildren, you finally "got it all together."

I'll never forget that fall day when Mama called and said, "You've got a new daddy." In response to my excitement, she told me you had professed your faith in Christ, repented, and accepted the forgiving grace of God. You *were* a changed man. Wow! After sixty years, you were beginning to become the man you could be.

You finally raised your mast and set your sails with God at the controls of your life. You knew where the port was, and you could see the harbor lights. You talked of one regret — that you hadn't followed the advice of your memorable speech which ended with these famous lines of another author:

> *One ship drives east and another drives west*
> *With the selfsame winds that blow.*
> *'Tis the set of the sails and not the gales*
> *Which tells us the way to go.*

> (from *Winds of Fate* by Ella Wheeler Wilcox)

I'm writing this letter to say what I neglected to say while you were alive: Daddy, I love you. I know you suffered. You knew we suffered. I wish we could talk over the past, and sometimes I wish you could re-live your life. However, I don't think that would be your wish. Instead, I'll praise the Lord for the day you were re-born and began a new life. We had only ten years of the good life with you, but I have an inkling that heaven is full of laughter because you are there. Chances are you re-arranged the stairway to heaven and set the saints a-laughin' while you did it. You and Jabo have probably melted down the streets of gold and made chariots for a "heavenly 500" for all those, like yourself, who got in late. I expect you tried to pick some fleecy white clouds thinking they were cotton you could sell while the market is high.

Knowing how you loved the finer things of life and things you couldn't afford, I am happy thinking of you in a mansion with jasper walls and pearl and gold. I know the roof doesn't leak and you are forever comfortable. You probably asked an angel why your room wasn't made of pine.

And speaking of angels, I'm sure the heavenly choir gave you a royal welcome such as you had never heard. You forgot the past, had no regrets, and of course, no tears or pain. I imagine you frolicked, teased, told funny stories, laughed a lot, and made others laugh. And then, you are forever thanking your Master that you are the man you are. Right on, Daddy!

I'm not sad now. I'm happy for you.

It isn't coincidental that at your death your only worldly goods left in the possession of your children were two hats — a winter felt and a summer straw — which

speak to us of the man you were and the man you
became.

I loved you then and
I love you now.

My Portrait of You

If you have a friend
Who brings out in you
The best and the noblest
In all you say and do—
Who knows where you're from
And where you are at,
And sees your faults and yet
Loves you in spite of that—
Who laughs when you laugh
And weeps when you weep,
Listening to your feelings
As well as words you speak—
Such friends, I say, are rare
And yet the words above
Perfectly portray you,
Seen through my eyes of love.

Wiser Than the Teacher

Fresh out of college and ready to teach the world, I landed in a most unlikely place from which to reach stardom. A series of circumstances led me right back to the place I was born.

Between the time I started elementary school at two-room Blue Hill School and the time I returned to teach, many small schools, including Blue Hill, had been consolidated and moved to Red Lick. Since things had changed so much, the opportunity to teach English in grades seven through twelve actually excited and challenged me. Every family name was familiar even though my family left there permanently when I started the seventh grade. The classes were small, and the children, with rare exception, had great respect for their teachers.

Three of my students were my first cousins, and I lived in their home and rode the school bus with them and about sixty other students. It troubled me that I was only twenty-one. In one class there was a senior boy about six-feet, four inches tall who had not moved along with his class each year, so he was near my age. He was a good boy, eager to learn, and always responsive to a compliment. He helped reinforce my philosophy that a person learns well when he likes himself and that a teacher never teaches by intimidating. I was enjoying good rapport as the learning process was evident.

On one particular day, though, I had to turn a near tragedy into triumph. We had been studying the degrees of adjectives and adverbs, and the students were adept at stating them correctly. I would say the adjective *good*, for instance, and single out a student who was to respond with *good*, *better*, *best*. We did this for the greater portion of the class period. I concluded with the word *sick*, and pointed to six-feet-four Clem, who said with a smile, "sick, sicker, sickest."

I should have stopped then, but I suspected that few students would realize the degrees of *ill* were the same as *sick*, so I asked Clem to give the degrees of ill. After serious thought, with hesitations between each word, he drawled out, "ill, iller, dead." The students roared with laughter, and I thought Clem might respond with anger because no one likes to be laughed at when he thinks he's right. To pour oil on troubled waters, I concluded that he was expressing himself well and that those were indeed the degrees we think of when we have an illness. Also, I assured him, I would never forget him. To this day, whenever I'm feeling ill, I pray I will not go through the three degrees Clem suggested.

Marriage Takes Three

I once thought marriage took
Just two to make a go
But now I am convinced
It takes the Lord also.
And not one marriage fails
Where Christ is asked to enter
As lovers come together
With Jesus at the center.
But marriage seldom thrives
And homes are incomplete
Till He is welcomed there
To help avert defeat.
In homes where God is first
It's obvious to see
Those unions really work,
For marriage still takes three.

Dear Love on Our Anniversary

Dear Love on Our Twenty-fifth Anniversary,

I have lived with you longer than I lived without you, and I'm glad.

You know I never have liked the idea of making a big "to do" over twenty-fifth and fiftieth wedding anniversaries. Most people seem to do it just because it is the thing to do. I feel each day is a milestone in a marriage, so I'm not going to say anything to you on our twenty-fifth that I wouldn't say any other day.

If I were a silver-tongued orator, my gift to you would be the words of a grand and glorious speech that you could have printed and framed to hang on your office wall. But since I prefer heart-to-heart talks, I'll avoid poetic phrases and simply tell you how I feel about our relationship.

We can look back on twenty-five years and hold it in our memory as a package. It's easy to see our past, to reminisce, and in so doing many emotions emerge.

Picture albums fill many of our shelves to help us

remember. Our wedding day was beautiful, and we still resemble that couple in the pictures whose eyes were filled with hope. Our honeymoon trip was romantic and maybe a bit expensive. We really didn't have much money, but we had hope, romance, and love.

Now we have acquired some material things we hoped for, and we still have hope, romance, love, and even more loved ones. I see our lives together as a garden. In our garden we have planted many good things. Some have flowered, and some have borne fruit.

We knew storms would come; we knew weeds would grow; and we knew we would always have to work in our marriage garden. I feel now that our relationship is stronger than ever and more beautiful because we have been weeding as we have gone along. I call it weeding after the wedding.

And more than that, it's still springtime, so we must plant more flowers that will bloom in the summer and fall yet to come.

We can hold each other when the winds blow. We can walk and talk together as we share our love and pull the weeds.

And who could be more admiring of what we have than you and I?

We have done it together, and we've only just begun.

I love you more now than I did when we started, and I will love you more tomorrow than I do today.

> So let the love grow,
> I love you so.

My Christmas Love

Here's my September song
That ran into October:
I love you more and more
Now that summer is over.
Here's November's refrain
Sung to the tune of Thanksgiving:
My love for you grows stronger
As does my love of living.
Christmas is memory time,
Yet I cannot remember
When I have loved you more
Than during this December.
Though Christmas soon must end
With seasonal fireside cheer,
Yet love observes no season.
I'll love you more next year.

Mum Isn't the Word

On a crisp morning in early November, we began what seemed to be an ordinary day. It didn't end that way.

My husband and I had breakfast together and watched a segment of the morning news on TV. After he left for his office, I poured my second (or was it third) cup of coffee and walked to the dining room window which gave a view of the front yard and street.

While standing there sipping my coffee, I did a panoramic "take" of all the neighbors' houses, the water tower, the school smoke stack, the unraked leaves, the pot holes in the streets, and the birds in the air, on the power lines, and in the trees. My heart was thrilled as I saw children skipping, running, and stumbling along to school. What a refreshing sight. It seemed as if the world was okay: my neighbors were safe, the water tower was serving its purpose, the wind was playing with the leaves, and the children were playing with each other. The birds seemed contented because the sun was shining and they enjoyed its warmth as they prepared for their journey south.

I too was contented and ready to start my day. My coffee was finished, and it was time for me to stop daydreaming and start preparing for dinner guests.

Suddenly my telescopic eyes focused on my own yard, and, closer yet, directly below the window where I was standing. I looked the distance from the garage door on my left to the front entrance on my right, which is about seven large shrubs (with spaces) wide. It was the spaces that caught my eye. Five years ago I had planted beautiful chrysanthemums (mums) in shades of gold and bronze, and they had grown to their crowning glory. During August, September, and October, they were as large as the shrubs and completely filled the spaces with brilliant color. They really put on a show.

What I saw (or didn't see) led me to believe I wasn't awake. Had we hit the snooze alarm; was I dreaming? If so, the first part of the dream was beautiful. If not, where were the mums? There were holes between each shrub, and the loose dirt didn't seem to be covering anything.

My adrenalin started to flow and, as usual, action followed. I telephoned my husband's office and, since he wasn't there, I unloaded on his secretary. She offered sympathy and said she would have him call me. In about ten minutes he called. "My secretary says you are upset," he said.

"Do you have any idea what happened to the plants between the shrubs in the front yard?" I responded loudly.

I didn't say "mums" because he's not famous for knowing the names of plants.

"Of course. Calm down and maybe sit down and certainly quiet down. They were frozen, so I thought it was about time to pull them from the ground."

"Dummy," I said impatiently, "you pull up marigolds and *trim* mums. I spent five whole years getting those plants to such a beautiful stage, and what do I have? Nothing. Why didn't you ask me before you did such a stupid thing?"

"I'll get you new ones, and they will be in the ground today," he insisted.

"I don't want new ones," I sobbed. "Many years are required to produce those enormous roots. Besides, you know we're having guests for dinner tonight."

Not knowing what to do with a hysterical wife on the other end of the telephone, he simply hung up.

Still flooded with anger and energy after surveying the situation, I went outside to contemplate a course of action. Soon I discovered a mound of neatly stacked "dead mums" with huge balls of dirt on the roots. There they were — all ready for the trash haulers. What a find! I hurried inside the garage and got the shears to trim away the dead stems. Then, lovingly, I lifted each big ball of dirt, held together by five-year-old roots, and placed it in the space it had been before.

Tired from the effort, I stood to rest before packing the dirt around the roots, when what to my wondering eyes should appear but my husband driving in our driveway. With a surprised look, he said, "The trash haulers came early today, didn't they?" I was about to give him the silent treatment, or maybe a shovelful of dirt in his face, when he opened the trunk of the car and lifted out several boxes of mums ready to be planted. His boyish look of relief and genuine love melted my anger. I dropped my shovel and, with mutual forgiveness wrapped in a big hug and a kiss, we decided once and for all that "Mum isn't the word."

More Like A Son

"More than a son-in-law,"
Is what we often said
During that glad occasion
When you our daughter wed.
Since then we've been thankful
That you were the choice one
To be our daughter's husband,
And to us, like a son.
We speak of you with pride
And with music in our voice,
For you're part of our family
And that makes us rejoice.
How fortunate for us
That your choice of a wife
Permitted us to be
The in-laws in your life.

With Love to My Daughter

Dear Daughter,

All girls are daughters, and even though many eventually become mothers, they never cease being daughters.

I am writing to you, my lovely daughter, on Mother's Day. Yes, I know this is a switch from tradition. You have always sent me the most beautiful flowers and gifts and loving cards in expression of your love for me. I always feel undeserving, and I become sentimental and weepy-eyed. You made me a mother for the first time. and I am proud to claim the title.

About midway through my pregnancy with you, the doctor ordered x-rays, thinking there were good indications I would have twins. The tests showed only one baby, but revealed improper development of your skeletal system. A second set of x-rays confirmed the first report. What was I to do with four and one-half more months of expectancy?

My faith was being tested. Your dad and I proclaimed once again our faith in God and on a very special evening we knelt in our living room and prayed. The Holy Spirit ministered to us and made our faith whole. We claimed all the promises of God and trusted Him as never before. Although I still had to dismiss doubts from my mind occasionally, our worry ceased, and I knew then that God was doing His work in us. But self-pity still plagued me, and I needed a daily cleansing. And each time I was scheduled for my regular visit to the doctor, whom I could have hated for telling me such a thing, I fought an inner battle. But on the other hand, the story wouldn't be so beautiful if he hadn't told me.

On May 28, about noontime, a nearly hysterical doctor announced to two new parents, "It's a beautiful girl and she is perfect." He seemed unable to believe it had happened. With tears of joy, we expressed our faith to him and then said aloud, "Thank you, God."

God truly had performed a miracle! In fact, He performed more than one miracle.

Having a child is always a miracle!
For God helping us to overcome hate and fear
helped us to maintain our sanity!
We exercised our faith by saying and believing —
"Thy will be done."

To those who want to explain away anything that appears to be a miracle of physical healing I've often said, "Our God can change things." He certainly proved His power by making you whole and filling you with a special gift of music.

When you were about three years old, you wandered

from our house to the church next door. Soon we heard beautiful piano music wafting from the windows. Upon investigation, we found our little girl standing on "tippie toes," reaching up to the piano keys. You seemed to be using all your fingers, and the songs were recognizable. We were overjoyed and stood in awe of your performance.

I'm not writing to re-tell your life to you, however. I'm writing to tell you how much you mean to me.

"Little girls are the nicest things that happen to people," wrote Alan Beck. His essay *What Is a Girl?* filled me with such anticipation and excitement that I framed it and hung it on your wall as a reminder of what was in store for me as a mother of a baby girl angel.

As the weeks turned into months and years, I learned firsthand the truth of his insightful essay; but I also learned some things his essay hadn't told me.

Little did I know that a girl angel stomps like an elephant, sings like a bird, climbs like a monkey, runs like a gazelle, flutters like a butterfly, slithers like a snake, eats like a pig, has the stubbornness of a mule, the slyness of a fox, and is as cuddly as a kitten.

She slams doors, hates boys, loves boys, messes up your house, puts mud pies on your porch, spills your perfume, cuts her hair in a crescent shape, dresses in your old clothes, loves dolls that have only one eye, and greets arriving guests in the nude.

Later I learned that teen-age girl angels are different from little girl angels. They cry a lot and laugh a lot for no apparent reason. They think mothers and daddies were created only to supply them with money. They listen to strange music and wear weird clothes, make-up, and perfume. The boys they claim as friends all have motorcycles or unsafe cars.

From the time you were little, whenever the flutter of your angel wings would cease temporarily, at least once a day, I would see how special God had made you. He blended together just the right combination of mischief, impatience, uncertainty, likes, dislikes, understanding, misunderstanding, ingenuity, clumsiness, creativity, thoughtfulness, truthfulness, thankfulness, tenderness, and, above all, the ability to love to make you the perfect addition to our family.

Your hugs and kisses and words of love always put a bit of "angel shine" in my day.

I'm sure I'm not a perfect mother because I'm not a perfect person, but becoming that has been my goal. I don't want to reflect on my imperfections, but on your possibilities.

Your possibilities are unlimited, and I know you will always find expression for the beautiful music God has put within you. And just as you have great musical possibilities, you, too, have the great heart to express love.

Dianne, when you announced you loved Steve and were planning to marry, we rejoiced with you because loving and being loved are heavenly. We told you before you married that the blending of two lives into harmonious living doesn't "just happen." Always respect each other, and show your love and respect in deeds of kindness. Never cease to have a good sense of humor seasoned with a lot of laughter. There will be tears, but they evaporate and later fall back as blessings on your garden of life.

Keep the flowers of love, joy, and peace in bloom to brighten stormy days because they are sure to come. Don't let a day end without touching and saying to each other, with feeling, I love you.

I am happy that you have a home, a wonderful husband, and a lot of love. Someday you will be a mother, and you will have even more love to share.

For now, and forever, I say to my daughter, I love you, I really love you.

Mom

You're Great

Just being yourself,
Open, kind and true,
Without pretentious airs,
Has drawn me close to you.
Your gift of listening
Brings out in me
The person I always
Wanted to be.
Your love of laughter
And your gift of praise
Inspire many friends
In countless ways.
Just being your plain self.
Is a noble trait.
It makes me think of you
As somebody great.

Say a Good Word

Four-year-old Michael elevated his grandpa to the status of a king with only a sentence.

Grandpa, a tree farmer, took Michael with him to cut Christmas trees to sell and to dig live (rooted) trees to be transplanted. Dressed in heavy clothing and warm boots for the cold and sloppy December weather, they drove the pick-up truck to the brink of safety, parked it, and walked into Grandpa's Christmas tree forest. Being in Grandpa's forest was a thrilling adventure for young Mike. He gazed in wonder at the huge swaying trees, perhaps seeing them as giants and monsters and imagining the whistling wind as voices. After a brisk walk, they selected a spot to begin the job of "tree digging." That was where daydreaming ended and work began.

Grandpa dug diligently, and Mike worked with great determination. As they finally released the tree's roots from the earth, each looked at the other with a satisfied expression. "Grandpa, you're the best tree-digger in the whole world," Michael said. In that magical moment the proud grandpa dropped his digging equipment, forgetting about the tree, and held his grandson close to him saying, "Mike, you make me feel like a king."

It was at a Christmas gathering that our son elevated his dad to royalty. Among the many relatives gathered for the festivities and gift exchange were six children under six years of age. The house was a clutter of boxes and bows and paper and toys. The noise factor was high, but not high enough to drown out a loud sob from one of the little boys who couldn't make his airplane work. He screamed us to silence, and his loving father took him and his airplane in his arms. The child was consoled momentarily, but the father didn't make any headway on repairing the toy. At that crucial moment, my son, Dwight, walked to the center of the disaster area and said to his uncle, "Let my dad fix it; he can do anything."

Sometimes we feel as great putting a crown of glory on someone else as we do in wearing one. So today is a good day to say a good word.

Thanks, Michael! Thanks, Dwight!

You're Someone Special

From every housetop
I'd like to shout it,
"Someone dearly loves you,
And don't you doubt it."
Were I a skywriter,
I'd write against the sky,
"I know one who loves you,
And how much and why."
I'd whisper in your ear
A message overdue,
"You're somebody special
Because someone loves you."
If you should ask of me
The one name on my tongue
Of those who love you best,
I'd say, "I'm that someone!"

Dear Son, With Love

Dear Son,

Every so often, especially on Mother's Day, I get a select card from you expressing your deep emotion and love for me. My mind holds the memories of your many cards, gifts, flowers, and acts of kindness, and I am sentimental with those memories.

You made me the mother of a son for the first time, and I was elated when the doctor said, "It's a boy." You weren't "just a boy," you were our very special boy, and we loved you even before you were born because your dad and I loved each other. You were born into a very secure nest, warm with love and a sister just waiting to be your playmate.

You were a happy, healthy baby who loved to be loved. You liked to sit in our laps, cuddle, and have us read books and tell stories to you. When the story ended you would always say, "Now, tell me a story about the 'olden days' when you were little."

When you were three months old, we were upset to

discover you had allergies that caused asthma. We seldom discussed the matter except in prayer, however, and you never seemed to know you had a problem. We will be forever grateful to God for enabling some good doctors help you overcome the ailment completely by the time you were twelve. God proved His power again.

Why shouldn't we thank God? We held you in our arms in front of the altar of the church and dedicated you to Him. At the same time, we promised to teach you and live before you the principles of Christ, which we have tried to do.

I have tried to be a perfect parent, but because I'm not a perfect person I have failed. I've done the best I know to do, however, and I love being a mother.

I love being the mother of a boy who has become a man. Now that you have accomplished so many things, I like to recall your boyhood days.

In his essay *What Is a Boy?* Alan Beck said that "between the innocence of babyhood and the dignity of manhood we find a delightful creature called a boy."

It's strange to think of you as a creature, but you certainly are a composite of many creatures I have observed.

I learned from you that boys possess chameleonlike qualities with some magical element. A boy can be singing like a lark one minute and fighting like a tiger the next. He can yodel sweetly from the top of a swaying tree and return to the ground as a vampire bat. He is a king, a slave, a teacher, a student, a cowboy, an Indian. And he knows how to lasso your heart.

With the eagerness of a beaver, the speed of a gazelle, and the slyness of a fox, he pursues whatever he wants to do. When called on to perform a task he may growl like a bear, hiss like a snake, and move like a snail.

Girls pursue them. Teachers tolerate them. Moms and dads adore them. Whenever you are enjoying a quiet moment, he needs to talk; but when you need to talk to him, he is nowhere to be found.

Boys can be beautiful, wise, helpful, hopeful, inconsiderate, loud, imaginative, enthusiastic, teasing, clumsy, and they are almost always hungry.

A boy sees the value in a bird feather, a nut, a rusty nail, a bottle cap, a piece of string, seeds, buttons, bits of plastic, a coin, a dog's tooth, and other unnamed items that are usually sticky and yukky, and so he usually comes home with an assortment that makes his pockets bulge.

When a boy is tired and his alibis have gone down the drain with the bath water, he is an angel. His halo shines even though it is sometimes tilted, and his smile, loving words, and tender hugs and kisses assure his parents that God really knew how to make a boy angel.

As a young boy, you were loving and kind, filled with energy and laughter and the unexpected. Some neighbors who played the role of grandparents to you always called you "sweet little innocent Dwight." You were a devilish, rugged, playful boy, who showed much love and affection. All this is true also in your manhood.

It has been said that "still waters run deep," and that typifies you. We have always sensed a special greatness about you that is sure to show. It isn't coming all at once, but with your sense of honesty and truth you are going to become one of the world's greatest men. You have always talked of house and home and children, and we call you a dreamer.

Your dreams are coming true, and you are realizing it was good to have dreamed. Our prayer for you is that you will never settle for second best and that you will make the most of each of life's situations. Always express your love and remain tender-hearted and sympathetic. Don't compromise right for wrong under any conditions and you will never lose sleep because of a guilty conscience. One of your great attributes is helping others, and we believe God rewards you for your helpfulness.

You are a very gifted young man, and we know music and the love for music is within you. Life really can be a symphony, and we believe your part will be in harmony. Sing and laugh as you plant seeds of love, kindness, and faith.

I love you so much I can't seem to find enough ways to show it. And so, in addition to finding ways to show my love, I want to say to you, my darling son, in all kinds of times, no matter what, no matter when, I love you, I love you, I love you.

Mom

He Promised Love

God has not promised
Life's journey will be
A rose garden stroll
From stumbling blocks free.
For trust is learned
In valleys of wrath,
And faith is tested
On a mountainous path.
But God has promised
On steep uphill trails
Where night boasts no stars
His presence will not fail.
And He promised love
And that He'll be near,
And walk with us through
Dark valleys of fear.

Medicine for Fear

Steven needed a physician when he developed a fever and other symptoms that wouldn't go away with his mother's tender loving care. His only other visits to the doctor's office had been for routine checkups and shots that are required for a robust start in life. Those times had faded from his memory. Steven was definitely robust, very gabby, and slightly afraid as he sat with his mother in the doctor's waiting room at the tender age of three.

Hoping to calm his fears, his mommy selected an interesting magazine from the rack, and she and Steven began to turn the pages and talk and laugh. It was difficult for Steven to pay attention to magazine pages, however, when the door to "who knew where" was opening as frequently as the pages were turning. A blonde nurse called for Cynthia, who was only a babe in arms. The loving parents carried Cynthia through the open door. Steven watched as the door closed behind them. Before he could breathe a sigh of relief, a hurting scream came from the deep, dark chasm of the inner-sanctum.

Suddenly the door opened and a different nurse came for another person. This was repeated several times, and each patient followed the nurse into the mysterious never-never land. Although not everyone screamed, it seemed as if no one ever returned. In his state of uncertainty, Steven began turning the pages of the magazine faster and without looking as he turned. His chatter became a series of questions to which he didn't await an answer.

Again the door opened, and a lovely, stately black nurse with a very soft voice called for Steven. He appeared startled. He had never encountered a person with skin that dark, so he was even more frightened and unsure. In a brief moment, an eternity to a three-year-old, Steven drew upon his young psyche and spoke with the wisdom of a thirty-year-old. He stood with confidence, reached for his mother's hand, walked toward the black nurse, looked directly at her, and said, "You know what? You look like chocolate pudding, and I love chocolate pudding."

With fears vanished, he proceeded to follow the nurse.

Footprints

The Lord appeared unto me
In a vision while I slept.
"Look back at life," He said.
"I've walked with you each step."
I saw His steps and mine
Went side by side for miles;
Yet only my steps entered
Deep valleys full of trials.
I was convinced those prints
Weren't His but my own steps.
"Lord, why was I forsaken
Just when I needed help?"
He said, "Footprints weren't yours
In dark valleys of life.
That's when I lifted you
And carried you through strife."

Take as Needed for Aggravation

Valium was only a word to me until I attended a neighborhood coffee klatch a few years ago. About twenty-five middle-class women were gathered on a warm and beautiful spring day to enjoy each other and celebrate the end of winter. Most of the women were under age forty-five, and all looked great and seemed happy. I heard about the marvelous accomplishments of their offspring, and it seemed as if all the women's children were excelling in everything.

I had been talking with one young mother only briefly when she hastily set down her cup and announced, "I'll be right back. I need to run home for a minute."

"Is there something wrong?" I asked.

"I forgot my valium," she responded, "and with all this coffee, I'll need it more than ever."

She didn't have to go home because another woman who overheard the conversation said, "Oh, don't leave; I have some in my purse, if five milligrams will do." The transaction was made.

I was disturbed by what I had heard and seen, but I didn't know exactly why. I did know, though, that it is usually at these coffee "get-togethers" that I hear mothers complaining about the awful problem of drug abuse among teenagers.

The woman who took her valium along with her coffee announced, as if she needed to explain, that her doctor prescribed this medication to help her cope with her family. She confided that she was grouchy, irritable, and nervous without it. Also, she said, her husband was taking her tablets, and he was much easier to live with.

Some time later, I saw my doctor about a very painful neck and shoulder ailment, for which he prescribed five milligrams of valium to be taken every six hours as needed for *aggravation*.

When I read those words on the pill bottle, I was too angered to take the first one for fear I would be aggravated forever. I called my doctor and told him I was sure he had made a mistake. "Don't you remember?" I said, "I came to you with a painful neck and shoulder condition. You gave me something for aggravation." He assured me I had the right medication. And I believed him until he called me by the name of the woman I had met at the coffee klatch.

We Can Go Home

There's truth in the thought,
"You can't go home again,"
But it's partly false
And always has been.
In our thoughts and dreams
We go home every day
To that treasured spot
That seems not far away.
Though miles come between
When the years have flown,
Yet with the speed of light,
Our memory takes us home.
The eye of memory sees
Some dear familiar face,
Or we touch a tree and sense
We never left that place.

God's Magic

The dream I had was vivid, action-packed, and scary. In the dark hours of a cold winter's night I awoke my husband and, with trembling voice, related to him the horror of the dream that had awakened me.

"You've had a nightmare," he insisted. "Now why don't you try to go back to sleep, for your sake as well as mine."

When I told him what my brother and sister-in-law were experiencing in my dream, he realized I would not go back to sleep easily. He suggested we pray for them. We prayed with great urgency that God would be present with our relatives who lived thousands of miles away. I recall the helplessness I felt, along with a twinge of superstitious uncertainty. Nevertheless, peace came to us as we petitioned our God who never sleeps, and we were asleep shortly thereafter.

Mid-morning the following day I called my brother's home and received no answer. When I called his office, his secretary said he would not be in that day, so I resigned myself to wait and hope to reach him later. Anxiety and peace somehow inhabited my mind at the same time, so I was in a constant state of prayer about a series of circumstances I had experienced only in a dream. *When will this end?* I thought to myself.

A few days later my brother called to explain what had happened to his family in the past few days. I listened in awe as he repeated my dream in the exact sequence I had told it to my husband.

What I dreamed had actually happened in the high mountain country of Colorado where babies are born light. In mid-afternoon of February 4, 1963, my sister-in-law Evelyn, a woman beyond the average age for giving birth, began labor for her fifth child. Hurriedly my brother Winston drove Evelyn the twenty-five miles to a small hospital in Salida, Colorado, where the family doctor met them and insisted that the father scrub and watch this birth, since he hadn't observed the others. The doctor suggested it would put a stop to future pregnancies.

When Evelyn's labor became intense, the doctor thought perhaps the baby was in a breech position, but soon the baby's head came into view and everyone was relieved. The child's upper torso was exceptionally large, however, so a surgical procedure was required to allow the five-pound baby boy to fit through the birth canal. Finally the infant took his first breath. The doctor expressed some concern when the baby's first gasp of air didn't cause him to turn the lively pink color of newborns, and he also commented about the child's large chest.

An attentive medical staff performed a variety of functions to help the "little fella" along. The attending physician said he would not leave and, with a few encouraging words, sent the father home to be with his other children.

Early the next morning, Winston received the grim news that his baby boy was not doing well and that the exhausted doctor had been relieved by his elder partner. When Winston arrived at the hospital the unfamiliar doctor approached him and said, "I believe we should let this baby die. Nature has made a mistake."

"What is the mistake?" Winston asked.

"The digestive system seems to be undeveloped," the doctor replied.

"What can we do?"

"Let him die."

"I won't take that for a last word."

"I'm sorry," the doctor said.

After this dialogue the anguished father called a pediatrician he knew in Colorado Springs and, with the assistance of a neighbor, took the very ill, bluish baby and started the ninety-eight-mile journey by car. They would have to cross three high and treacherous mountain passes which were usually impassable at this time of year.

At the highest altitude of Trout Creek Pass, the neighbor holding the baby announced that the child was near death. At the second pass, she declared he was dead.

Winston drove at law-breaking speed and arrived at St. Francis Hospital with a barely alive baby. The pediatrician, a surgeon, and others met them, and within thirty minutes the baby was in surgery.

After several hours, a nurse reported to a very tired father, who had spent the hours in prayer, that the baby was alive and that doctors would soon provide a full report.

"We found an underdeveloped diaphragm with a hole in its middle," the doctor finally reported to him. "We stretched and stitched it and pulled the ribs together tightly with synthetic strings to hold the diaphragm together. One lung was never inflated and the other only partially inflated. Besides these problems, the heart was located where the liver should be, and the spleen, liver, one kidney, and part of the stomach were in the left chest. We did all we could today, but he'll need more surgery if he survives."

When I told my brother about my dream and our prayers for him and his family, we both felt the awesome sense of wonder that always accompanies miracles. We ended our phone conversation by agreeing that the baby's only hope was intercessory prayer, which I promised we would continue to offer in generous amounts.

The struggle to live had just begun for baby Roy. Our phone lines and prayer lines were very busy for a long time thereafter. The rest of the story has been revealed over a period of years.

After several weeks of touch and go, doctors decided the baby needed a complete change of blood. Since his home would be high in the mountains, he needed blood from someone acclimated to an altitude of eight thousand feet or above. Inmates at the Colorado State Reformatory at Buena Vista willingly gave more than enough blood for this innocent baby who was fighting for life.

His color improved after the blood transfusion and the crisis seemed to be over. Doctors suggested that the exhausted father go home and spend time with his wife, who was still in the hospital suffering from phlebitis, and the rest of his family.

That news appealed to him, so he reluctantly left the baby and started home over the mountains. Between the second and third pass he was beckoned to the side of the road by a highway patrolman. He knew this meant trouble. After confirming Winston's identity, the officer told him his baby was gravely ill and that he must return to Colorado Springs.

After the patrolman left, Winston laid his head on the steering wheel and cried helplessly, "Lord, this very minute I give up this child to You. I haven't been able to cuddle him, his mother hasn't held him, yet we love him. I don't know how to pray, what to do, or where to go. I truly give him back to You and, from the deepest ache in my soul, I say now, not my will but Yours be done. Thank You, Lord!"

Toward the end of February this small "miracle boy" came home to a family that didn't know him but loved him. Despite his frail condition, he added a new sparkle to that home. He belonged there. Nearly every night his daddy held him on a pillow and walked the floor all night to get him to rest. There were days when his bowels and kidneys would not function. Breathing was often difficult. The special attention and care he received made him highly responsive to love. He began smiling and cooing, and the family maintained hope.

Another crisis came in May when he suffered a collapsed lung. Although the situation was critical, before leaving for the hospital in Colorado Springs, the whole family gathered around their precious little survivor-fighter and prayed. They believed God had a definite purpose for his life, and God assured them that He did.

The same loving doctors who had helped him before took him to surgery again. They found and repaired a herniated diaphragm which had allowed his stomach to push into his chest and cause a collapsed lung. Also during surgery another kidney was found atop the lung and had to be put in place.

This tough little boy had now survived his second major surgery in his first three months, and he was making great strides toward good health.

Six months later the family decided to go to Phoenix to enjoy a warmer climate and to spend Christmas with relatives. Before they reached Phoenix, however, Roy began turning blue. Winston called ahead to the Good Samaritan Hospital and asked that they contact a thoracic specialist. Upon arrival they were greeeted by a pediatric thoracic surgeon who "just happened" to be on call that night.

Immediately they began working on the baby. The surgeon asked the parents to allow him to experiment with a process that he and a doctor in Washington, D.C., were developing. Winston and Evelyn gave their permission and surgery proceeded.

After surgery the doctor explained, "Your baby's diaphragm had a hole in it that was causing many complications. I used Marlex gauze to patch it, and I believe it will be perfect." He also told them this was only the third time he had used this procedure.

The "much prayed for" baby made a fantastic recovery and, by this time, all who were involved had exercised their faith to the point there was no way anyone would give up or show any sign of waning faith. The road ahead for this little fighter and his family would not be without more traumas, but they all knew God was present at every turn. Hope and faith were hand in hand and a new sense of the power of prayer had emerged for the whole family. It seemed as if this tiny child who had had very few well days was aware God was caring for him and his family.

A few years later Winston was transferred to Washington, D.C., in another of God's wonderful miracles which always seem like magic. The surgeon who worked on the Marlex gauze experiment with the doctor in Phoenix knew Roy's case history and was pleased to take him as a patient.

The two surgeons collaborated on his condition and when Roy was eight years old they felt he should return to Phoenix so the surgeon who had successfully closed the diaphragm could operate to expand the rib cage, which had been tied so tightly to hold the diaphragm. This was done with precision and no ill effects. The surgeon announced that the diaphragm was in perfect condition and everything about the child appeared to be normal.

Magic met Roy and his family at every turn. I call it magic because of the smoothness with which God carries out His miracles. When we least expect them and in ways we can't dream of, God works miracles.

This miracle baby is now a twenty-one-year-old miracle man who is in college and working toward a medical career.

All who agonized and prayed for him through his

many crises know the power of prayer, and Roy knows God saved him for a very special purpose.

We have learned that the burdens that bear down on our souls are sometimes the magic of God.

A Letter From Helen Steiner Rice

Helen Steiner Rice was a friend of our family and, on rare occasions, would leave her apartment to visit us. On one Thanksgiving Day she came to our home in Mt. Washington, a Cincinnati suburb, and shared with us many things about her life. Being in her presence made us aware of her greatness as well as her humility. She never missed an opportunity to say a good word for the Lord.

I wrote to her a short time after her Thanksgiving visit and asked her to be the guest speaker at a women's convention. I'll never forget her interesting reply.

> I don't accept speaking engagements. All that I have to say is in my writings, and I want to reach more people, in more places, and in more ways, but business is very brutal and publishers are insatiable at times. It is not easy to do something in a *simple, uncomplicated way for the Lord.*
>
> I recently answered a letter one young school girl fan wrote me in this way: "Here's a little secret . . . I DO NOT WORK FOR GIBSON. I WORK FOR

GOD! I just let Gibson think I work for them so I can use them as a channel . . . and I am willing to make PROFITS for GIBSON in order to make PROPHETS for GOD. Writing these inspirational poems is a VOCATION, an AVOCATION, and a DEDICATION with me. I do not take extra payment for my inspirational work . . . that would rob it of all meaning. GOD GIVES US EVERYTHING and only by HIS GRACE can we do anything at all . . . for without HIM we are weak and we would fall . . . so, as I say, SEEK YE FIRST THE KINGDOM OF GOD AND THE WORLD IS YOURS AND ALL THAT IS IN IT."

So, my very best to the family and thanks for writing. It was SO NICE TO HEAR FROM YOU.

> With fond regards,
> Sincerely,
> Helen Steiner Rice